VIPERS

BY: ERIC ETHAN

Gareth Stevens Publishing
MILWAUKEE

For a free color catalog describing Gareth Stevens' list of high-quality books, call 1-800-542-2595 (USA) or 1-800-461-9120 (Canada). Gareth Stevens' Fax: 1-414-225-0377.

Library of Congress Cataloging-in-Publication Data

Ethan, Eric.
  Vipers / by Eric Ethan.
    p. cm. — (Fangs! an imagination library series)
  Includes index.
  Summary: Describes what various types of vipers look like, what they eat, where they can be found, how they defend themselves, the danger from their bites, and the outlook for their future.
  ISBN 0-8368-1432-0
  1. Viperidae—Juvenile literature. [1. Poisonous snakes.
2. Snakes.] I. Title. II. Series: Ethan, Eric. Fangs! an imagination library series.
QL666.069E863   1995
597.96—dc20   95-19263

Published in 1995 by:
Gareth Stevens Publishing
1555 N RiverCenter Drive, Suite 201
Milwaukee WI 53212 USA

Original Text: Eric Ethan
Series Design: Shari Tikus
Cover Design: Karen Knutson
Photo Credits: Pages 5, 17, and 21 © Joe McDonald; Pages 7, 9, 11, 13, and 19 © James Carmichael; Page 15 © Brian Kenney

Printed in the United States of America
     4 5 6 7 8 9 99

TABLE OF CONTENTS

WHAT ARE VIPERS?

Vipers are the largest family of poisonous snakes in the world. There are over one hundred and fifty types of vipers. They include the most dangerous snakes in the world.

Many snakes lay eggs. But most vipers give birth to small live baby snakes. The common name viper means to give birth to live young.

The saw-scaled or carpet viper of North Africa may be the deadliest snake in the world.

WHAT DO THEY LOOK LIKE?

All vipers have flat, wide heads shaped like triangles. They have small necks followed by larger bodies.

Vipers that spend most of their time on the ground have larger, heavy bodies. These vipers grow to 24-48 inches (60-120 cm) in length. Vipers that spend most of their time in trees are thinner and longer. They measure longer than 36 inches (90 cm) when fully grown.

All vipers have large, moveable fangs that are folded back against the top of their mouth when not in use. Their bodies are covered by flat tough plates called scales. Most viper scales have ridges running down the middle of them.

This gaboon viper of central Africa has a heavy body and a head shaped like a triangle.

WHERE ARE THEY FOUND?

Vipers are found in every part of the world except Australia and New Zealand. There are three types of vipers in the United States; Copperheads, Rattlesnakes, and Cottonmouths. Most vipers are found in Africa, Asia, and South America. This book talks about vipers found outside North America.

Vipers live in many different **habitats**. In the rain forests of South America and Africa vipers live in trees. In deserts and grassy areas vipers live on the ground.

In places where it is cold part of the year, vipers **hibernate** in dens. Dens are usually holes in the ground or in rocky areas. Where it is warm all year round, snakes do not hibernate. But they may have a den to go to.

The Russell's viper of Southeast Asia is very deadly.

SENSES AND HUNTING

All snakes are **predators**. This means they must hunt other animals to stay alive. Snakes cannot hear very well. And they can only see a short distance. In order to find their prey, snakes use special senses.

Each time a viper's tongue flicks out, it takes a sample of the air and ground around it. In the viper's mouth, the **Jacobson's organ analyzes** what the tongue picks up. This tells the viper what is around it.

An eyelash viper using its tongue to find prey.

Many vipers, called pit vipers, have small pits between the eyes and nose. These are called **loreal pits**. They help the snake to detect warm prey even at night. Some vipers do not have loreal pits. They must rely on their tongue and eyes to find prey.

Sometimes vipers ambush their prey. This means the snake waits in one place a long time until something it can eat comes near. Vipers will also hunt for food. Vipers that live in trees creep up on their prey very slowly. When hunting on the ground, some vipers can move very quickly over short distances. These can be very dangerous snakes.

Can you see the loreal pit between the eye and nose of this eyelash viper?

WHAT DO THEY EAT?

Vipers that live in desert or grassy areas catch most of their prey on the ground. They eat small **mammals** like rats and mice as well as lizards and other snakes. Vipers that live in trees often catch birds and lizards that climb trees.

Whatever vipers are able to catch they always eat it head first. This makes it easier to swallow large prey. The mouth of a viper can stretch large enough to swallow an animal bigger around than it is.

This white-lipped pit viper has caught a frog.

SELF-DEFENSE

Viper's most important form of self-defense is **camouflage**. Camouflage makes the snake difficult to see. If danger comes near, the viper will lay still until it goes away. If it has a chance the viper will move away quietly. Vipers want to save their **venom** for hunting.

Some vipers, like the saw-scaled viper of North Africa are very aggressive. They will attack if danger is near. Saw-scaled vipers have very strong venom and are said to be the most deadly snakes in the world.

Large birds, like hawks and eagles, are known to attack vipers. Sometimes other snakes prey on vipers, too. Because fully grown vipers are so dangerous, their main enemy is man.

*Gaboon vipers of central Africa
are well camouflaged.*

VIPER BITES

Viper bites are very serious. Nearly all viper's venom is strong enough to kill a human. Vipers inject venom through their fangs. Fangs are very sharp, hollow teeth. Vipers have larger fangs than any other snake. Fully grown these fangs reach 1/2-3/4 of an inch (1.3-1.9 cm). The fangs of the gaboon viper of central Africa have been measured at nearly 1-1/2 inches (3.8 cm). When not in use the viper's fangs are folded back against the roof of the snake's mouth.

Most of the time, vipers bite and release their prey. The viper's venom is very strong, and the animal does not go far after being bitten. When catching birds, vipers do not let go when they bite. If they did, the bird could fly too far for the snake to find again.

A rough-scaled bush viper about to strike.

UNUSUAL FACTS

The saw-scaled viper of North Africa puffs up its body and rubs its scales together as a warning. This makes a loud buzzing sound.

Vipers live farther north and south on the Earth than any other snake. The European adder has been found as far north as the Arctic Circle. Countries like Finland and England, not known for their poisonous snakes, report dozens of bites each year from the European adder.

The Russell's viper of India and Sri Lanka is far more of a danger than the cobra. The Russell's viper and saw-scaled viper, which live from India to the Middle East, kill more people than any other snakes.

The rhinoceros viper of central Africa.

THE FUTURE

Vipers that live in remote areas of the world like deserts and rain forests are the safest. Everywhere that vipers live close to man they have been hunted and killed. There are far fewer vipers like copperheads and rattlesnakes in the eastern United States than there once were.

The biggest threat to most vipers is habitat destruction. As forests are cut and open areas converted to farmland, vipers lose their place to live. Often the animals snakes hunt disappear first. Then the snake can no longer find enough food to live in the area.

GLOSSARY

analyze (AN a lize) - To separate something into its parts to study them.

camouflage (KAM 0 flazh) - Colors or patterns that helps an animal look like the ground around it.

habitat (HAB i tat) - The place where an animal is normally found.

hibernate (HI ber nate) - To spend the winter in a deep sleep.

Jacobson's organ (JAY kob sons OR gan) - A special pouch in a snake's mouth that analyzes what the tongue picks up.

loreal pit (LOR e all) - A small hole near a snake's nose that can see infrared light.

mammal (MAM el) - A warm-blooded animal that has a backbone.

predator (PRED a tor) - An animal that lives by killing and eating other animals.

venom (VE nom) - The poison of snakes.

INDEX

PLACES TO WRITE FOR MORE INFORMATION

American Society of Ichthyologists and Herpetologists
US National Museum
Washington, DC 20560

Copeia
American Society of Herpetologists
34th Street and Girard Avenue
Philadelphia, PA 19104

Herpetologists' League
1041 New Hampshire Street
Lawrence, KS 66044

Herpetological
1041 New Hampshire Street
Lawrence, KS 66044